From
Pillar
to
Post

From
Pillar
to
Post

A pictorial celebration of
Post Offices

John Spencer Gilks

Edited by Mike Esau

SLP

Silver Link Publishing Ltd

This book is dedicated to
Frank Paterson
for his consistent support and confidence in the idea.

First published in 2010

British Library Cataloguing in Publication Data

A catalogue record for this book is available from the British Library.

ISBN 978 1 85794 321 4

Silver Link Publishing Ltd
The Trundle
Ringstead Road
Great Addington
Kettering
Northants NN14 4BW

Tel/Fax: 01536 330588
email: sales@nostalgiacollection.com
Website: www.nostalgiacollection.com

All photographs were taken by the author unless otherwise credited.

Printed and bound in the Czech Republic

Aims to bring PO pictures to book

JOHN GILKS: Enveloped in his task

Title page A post van at **STAUNTON ON ARROW**, Herefordshire

Left The author as photographed and published by the *Ryedale Star* free newspaper on 5 March 1992 before setting out on his mammoth trip round the UK.

Opposite page The author relaxes outside **HAWNBY** Post Office near his home in North Yorkshire on 5 August 1992 prior to having a cup of tea in its garden across the road.

Contents

Introduction

Throughout my life – and I was born in 1932 – the staff who run the Post Offices have had a human face. Even today, the lady who generally brings my post will push a DVD, which is too big for my letter box, through the open window of my kitchen on to the table if I happen to be out. Real service!

But just as at seventy-seven I get set in my ways, so the Post Office – which has existed in some form since 1635 – needs to be examined from time to time and the wrinkles taken out of its appearance. Otherwise we could well sound the last post as email and other electronic means of communication undermine the system. In so doing, however, the balance has to be struck between profit and personality; esprit de corps is a valuable commodity and survives now on a grand scale in UK civilian life only in the Post Office.

A letter still costs the same to send, whether from Land's End to John o'Groats or from home to the next street, just as it did when Parliament sanctioned the policy in 1897 as one of Queen Victoria's Diamond Jubilee concessions. Moreover, it is delivered to your door, unlike in America, for example, where you have to make a journey to a box at the Post Office. However, according to the BBC TV news programme *Look North* on 1 August 2008 this policy has been challenged by the Post Office, which has announced that the

hamlet of Booze near Langthwaite in Arkengarthdale, North Yorkshire, will no longer receive post. The lane to the cottages, which is about one mile in length, is said to be too dangerous for staff to travel from a Health & Safety viewpoint. What is the highway authority doing about this? Is it coincidence that the announcement is made when residents are likely to be on holiday and newspapers are searching for copy? And is it really chance that the place selected has such an unusual and amusing name? The concern smacks more of a public relations agency than local van drivers. Perhaps it is fortunate that the site is in the actively democratic constituency of Richmond (Yorkshire), or near its boundary. Watch this space!

The uniform Penny Post dates from 1840, and the mail was carried between receiving houses – the precursor of the Post Office – by post boys who were expected to walk seventeen miles a day, seven days a week. The letter box, which first appeared at the roadside in 1852, is an item of street furniture seen everywhere in the UK and still bears the ciphers of the sovereigns from Victoria to Elizabeth II, not forgetting Edward VIII. Most of the boxes are in cast iron and have stood the test of time very well. No throwaway attitude here, and no money wasted on flashy new designs!

Apart from the pub, the Post Office has

◁ This view at **WINGHAM** in Kent, on the A257 Canterbury-Sandwich road, shows the link at that time between communications by letter and telephone, while the van waits to deliver and carry away the mail. It is 29 August 1990, a really sunny day, and all the windows in the house are open.

▷ The road to Booze in 2008, considered too dangerous for staff to travel along for Health & Safety reasons...

been the one surviving hub of village life. It has been the heart of the community. The postmaster or postmistress knows everybody's business. I once posted a film in Newcastleton on which I wrote the return address. On going back to the Post Office there later in the afternoon the postmistress remarked how far away I was from home! She also provided the useful information that my film would be taken on the down 'Waverley Express' to Edinburgh before going south, and I witnessed the postman loading a bag into the train. She also acts as a social worker and financial adviser to all.

The oldest active Post Office is at Sanquhar in Dumfriesshire, and dates from 1763. Some other early establishments are at Banbury (1836), Crathie, Aberdeen (1842), Dennington, Suffolk (1847), Edderton, Dingwall (1834), Guyhirn, Wisbech (1850s), King's Worthy, Hampshire (1845), Penshurst, Kent (1861), Potterspury, Towcester (1866), Shipton-under-Wychwood, Oxford (1845), Stoke Climsland, Callington (1839), Stoulton, Worcestershire (1850) and Wormshill, Sittingbourne (1847). Whereas the village school, railway station, bus stop, and even the church have withered away in many country places, until recently the Post Office has survived. In 2008 a Network Change Programme was implemented whereby some 2,500 of its national network of around 14,300 outlets were expected to be shut. It is time, therefore, to record the variety of Post Offices that we have enjoyed.

When standardisation is so much in vogue, when uniformity is considered a virtue, when one town centre appears more and more like another and when chain stores adopt common shop fronts for ease of identification, it is reassuring to look at a national network that, like people, retains individuality.

It was in September 1988 that I wrote to the Chairman of the Post Office with my idea, and met his representative the following August. Then followed a Letter of Authority to be shown in Post Offices to demonstrate that my intentions were honourable, a letter in their Newsletter inviting suggestions for visits, and even a fax from HQ to regional offices asking them to indicate places of unusual interest. I couldn't have wished for more cooperation, and much information was forthcoming, on which this book is based. I then met the archivist, Jean Farrugia, and was given free run of the picture library in London. Can I thank everyone for their trouble and for their patience; they must have wondered by now whether their time had been wasted. In most cases it has not been. I have journeyed with my camera and the results are for you to judge. How many of the Post Offices you see still give service I know not.

The pictures are set out by regions together with those in Scotland and Wales. An archive section in black and white drawn from the British Postal Museum & Archive, for which I am most grateful to Barry Atto and Garth Stewart, forms the spine of the book. I have taken the opportunity to focus also on Post Buses, post boxes and Travelling Post Offices on the railway, with a small section on each topic. Captions are longer where special events have occurred during my travels.

I would like to thank Peter Townsend of Silver Link Publishing and editor Will Adams for sponsoring my idea and taking it from text and picture to finished product, and Mike Esau for his editing skills. John Edgington has done the donkey work as usual with good grace. I have had the good fortune to have the company and advice of Gavin Mist and David Short on some of the early missions. Now on with the explorations!

John Spencer Gilks
Nawton
North Yorkshire

Post Offices in
The South and West

△ It seems appropriate to begin our exploration near the East Kent coast, prior to travelling west and north to finish up on the outer islands of Scotland.

The is the Post Office at **RUCKINGE** on the B2067 (to Hythe), east of Ham Street station on the Ashford-Hastings railway, on 30 August 1990. I am on my way to see the nuclear flask being brought across Romney Marsh from Dungeness power station.

▷ The following day I photographed a far more modern building housing both a butcher's shop and a Post Office – quite a new development at the time – in Bush Road at **STROOD** in the Medway towns of Kent.

△ This is **BARRINGTON** near Chard, Somerset, in the autumn of 1989.

◁ The superb location of this Post Office is **BERKELEY** in Gloucestershire. The date is 3 September 1990 and I'm staying with friends near Banbury. We are having a day out with lunch at a *Good Food Guide* restaurant in nearby Frampton.

▷ At the time of this 1991 photograph **BLEADON**, near Weston super Mare, was in the county of Avon. Previously it had been in Somerset and I believe it may have returned to that administrative fold. See how the church dominates the Post Office!

▷ *Inset* The Post Office at **BRATTON FLEMING** (a village once served by the Lynton & Barnstaple Railway), seen in March 1992, reminds us of the days when it was the agent for the National Savings Bank and the National Giro Bank. It is situated in the lonely hills north-east of Barnstaple in Devon on the fringe of Exmoor.

△ Just a few miles further east is **CHALLACOMBE** on the B3358 road from Exford. In March 1992 the Post Office and telephone box are joined by a modern petrol pump, vehicles being topped up in the street.

◁ The famous view down to the sea at **CLOVELLY** in Devon is punctuated by the Post Office in the foreground on the west side of the street. It is 13 March 1991, but could be a summer's day! I'm staying with friends in the Quantocks and taking them for a day out.

▷ The Post Office at **COSSINGTON**, north-east of Bridgwater in Somerset, doubles as a butcher's shop. It was photographed on 8 March 1991 as I made my way to the West of England. There had once been a station here on a former Somerset & Dorset Railway branch; British Railways closed it completely on 4 October 1954 but the track was still in position when I obtained a picture for my archive the following year.

◁ On 19 March 1997 I strolled round **DORCHESTER** (Dorset) and came across this fine building in the High Street. I had already seen a print of it in the Post Office archives and it looked quite unchanged over the years. I've just bought my first CD of an historic restoration – Stephane Grappelli with *Crazy Rhythm* – which proved to be very acceptable!

△ *Left* **DOWLISH WAKE** is a village south-east of Ilminster in Somerset. I was there on 15 March 1991.

△ *Right* It was an interesting day, starting from the motorway Travelodge on the M5 at Sampford Peverell, an unusual overnight location for me. Going across the Culm Valley and a succession of hilly byroads I came to **DUNKESWELL**, with ducks in the garden of the Post Office. I had been here on official business twenty years earlier (see page 25), and as you will find I later went to Luppitt before rain came on at Crewkerne and I phoned ahead to Summer Lodge at Evershot to partake of an excellent lunch, which made up for the weather. In the evening I was with a friend at Frimley in Surrey.

▽ Keeping in alphabetical order, we now reach **GARA BRIDGE**, which is in Devon, though I can find no mention of it in the *County Court Index to Parishes, Townships, Hamlets and Places.* This is my bible for locating Post Offices when seated before my computer and bereft of memory!

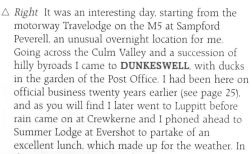

No such problem with this Post Office! As a result of my letter in *Counters Courier* for December 1989, Margaret Stanbury wrote to me from Inwardleigh in Devon where she was the sub-postmistress. She said that the Post Office was 'sited in a front room of a farmhouse. The agricultural activities still continue, trading under the name of Hillside Farm. We are one house with two addresses ... prior to becoming a farmhouse about 70 years ago it was an inn – the Sportsman's Inn – built by Lord Portland. He built inns each a day's ride apart, from his town house in the Square named after him in London to his country seat in Cornwall ... by building these inns it meant he could always stay the night at his own property and avoid hotel bills.'

I contacted Margaret Stanbury and she promised to bake me a cake if I included her unusual Post Office in my itinerary. This I did on 14 March 1991, with the desired result!

INWARDLEIGH is north of Okehampton in Devon, west of the A386. The village was featured in the national press during the Gulf War because a wedding there had to be postponed while the groom was posted abroad.

◁ *Far left* **LUCCOMBE** adjoins the Holnicote Estate high in the hills below Dunkery Beacon in Somerset and well south of Minehead. Access is gained from the A39 some miles east of the famous Porlock Hill, but care and concentration are needed by car. The date is 12 March 1991.

◁ *Left* Until I pursued my itinerary for this book I had not heard of **MONKOKEHAMPTON**, but here is its Post Office, near the more famous town in North Devon, on 14 March 1991.

◁ *Below left* As mentioned above I reached **LUPPITT** on the following day, again on the Post Bus route from Honiton discussed on page 24.

▽ **MORETON** in Dorset, however, was well known to me as having one of the best rail services hourly to and from Waterloo station in London, which for some years have been provided by fast modern electric trains. My visit was on 10 March 1992.

◁ **NUNNEY** is south-west of Frome in Somerset and I had bed and breakfast at Bridge House there on 7 March 1991, having seen the first lambs of spring.

▽ On 3 September 1990 I visited **PAINSWICK** in Gloucestershire and during my tour of the village I took this photograph. I'm on the same day out mentioned above, with friends who live near Banbury.

△ We cannot go much further west than **PENZANCE** in Cornwall, and according to the slide this picture was taken on Saturday 24 August 1991. I have no reason to believe otherwise, but it must have been supplied to me as my diary says that I was at home. Thus I must apologise for not giving the photographer due credit.

▽ The Post Office at **WESTONZOYLAND** is next door to the Sedgemoor Inn, commemorating the nearby battle that took place on the marshy ground between Wells and Glastonbury in Somerset in 1685.

◁ Mrs Knighton was surprised to see me when I called at her Post Office in the Dorset village that goes by the name of **WHITCHURCH CANONICORUM**! It's the first Post Office that I have entered through a door surrounded by vines. This was on 10 March 1992 and I had been encouraged to make my visit by her relative who ran the Post Office at Staintondale in North Yorkshire (see page 101 below).

▽ **WINKLEIGH** is on the B3220 Torrington-Crediton road in Devon and is not really near anywhere! I found it for this photograph on 21 October 1993.

WOOTTON FITZPAYNE (*inset*) is a village in the hills north of Charmouth in Dorset, while **WHEDDON CROSS** is high on Exmoor in Somerset where the B3224 from Lynton meets the A396 running from north to south over the hills, eventually to Tiverton. It is a suitable place to end our tour of the South and West.

Post routes and Post Buses

▽▷ These two maps show post routes from Manchester in 1807 and 1813, delineating the roads followed by the mail to and from London and on cross-country routes such as to Warrington and to Bradford. In addition there are the routes followed daily (and less frequently) by horse post and those used by foot messengers. Note that on the 1813 map armed horse posts have been introduced between Wakefield and Ferrybridge, south of Halifax, between Rochdale and Chorley, and between Blackburn and Skipton! A summer service has begun between Buxton and Leek.

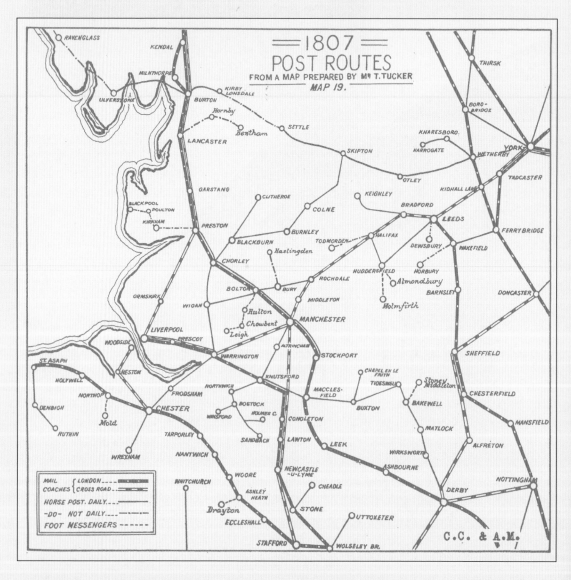

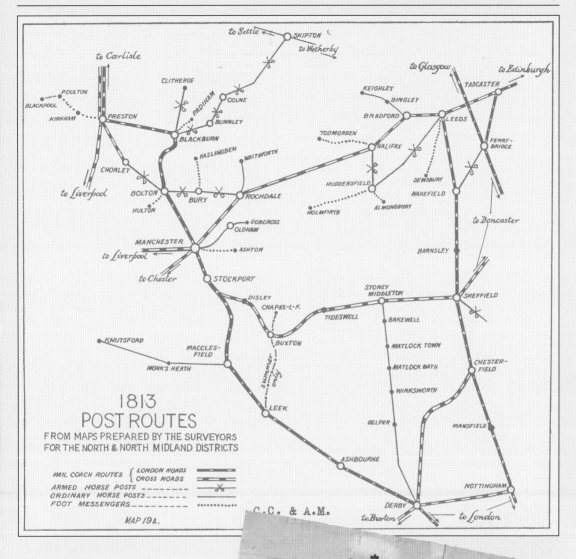

1813
POST ROUTES
FROM MAPS PREPARED BY THE SURVEYORS
FOR THE NORTH & NORTH MIDLAND DISTRICTS

MAIL COACH ROUTES { LONDON ROADS		
CROSS ROADS		
ARMED HORSE POSTS		
ORDINARY HORSE POSTS		
FOOT MESSENGERS		

MAP 19A.

On the 1st July next, a POST will be established TWICE-A-DAY, between NEWCASTLE and NORTH SHIELDS, to set out and return as follows :---

	H. M.	
To leave Newcastle	at 6 30	in the Morning.
To return to Ditto	at 1 15	in the Afternoon.
To leave Newcastle again	at 3 0	Ditto.
To return to Ditto	at 9 15	at Night.

Post-Office, Newcastle, 23rd June, 1824.

E. Walker, Printer, Newcastle.

▷ A notice announcing the times of a newly operated post between Newcastle-upon-Tyne and North Shields in 1824.

During 1967 steps were taken to introduce minibuses on certain GPO mail van services so as to offer a transport facility to the public in remote areas, and grants were to become available from local government for selected rural bus routes. Initially three services were operated. The first was from Penrith to Martindale in the Lake District of Cumbria, passing the famous Sharrow Bay Hotel on the way.

On 22 October 1970 I made my way to Honiton in Devon as Assistant Secretary of the Rural District Councils Association to experience travel on one of the routes. I recall that the Head Postmaster was concerned at the staff time involved in having to wash the bus every day, unlike the mail vans. Later on there were security problems with the conveyance of national insurance stamps to outlying Post Offices. But the idea was sound and some routes still survive. They provide an opportunity for tourists, particularly appealing to Americans, to venture up the drive to the manor house and to other locations that are normally off limits, but this aspect doesn't seem to have been exploited in the written publicity, understandably perhaps.

Routes D1 to D10 were in the North West.

Some buses seated ten or eleven people whereas others, such as those based on Alston and Brampton in Cumbria, carried a maximum of four. As we shall see from the illustrations, a private car and a Land Rover carried even fewer! The leaflet said that 'travelling by Post Bus offers the rare opportunity to explore the countryside in the company of local people, to experience the hustle and bustle of traditional market towns'. An unsung benefit to visitors was the fact that the routes were circular (or there and back), so it was almost impossible to get lost on the way. Some routes took two to three hours to complete.

The Post Office laid down the following conditions before starting a service:

- There should be a need (proven by a request from a local authority, parish council or a Women's Institute)
- It should not compete with any existing bus service
- It should fit in with postal operating requirements (including security) without being too circuitous for passengers
- If it runs at a loss it should be grant-aided under Section 34 of the Transport Act 1968.

◁△ The Post Bus waits outside the office in **DUNKESWELL** in Devon, on the author's journey on 22 October 1970. Another photo of the scene appears on page 14. Later in the day the driver kindly waited for me to photograph the bus en route across high ground near Dunkeswell, while the final view shows the bus waiting for passengers and mail in **LUPPITT**.

△ At the other end of England – in Northumberland – the Land Rover that acts as the Post Bus to Wooler takes a rest on Easter Monday 1983 by a barn in the **HAPPY VALLEY**.

▷ Road/rail co-ordination as envisaged by the Local Government Act 1972 is seen in practice at **CHATHILL** station in Northumberland on the evening of 10 June

1986. Under the second rule of the Post Office code outlined on page 24 the Post Bus could not operate from Bamburgh on Saturdays because United, the local bus operator, already held a licence for that day. The County Co-ordinator, John Wylde, could not understand why the connections were not made at Chathill at weekends until he realised that a different driver was likely to be involved each week and had

not been advised why he turned at the station. Such are the benefits of centralisation!

I think it is worth two pictures of this operation. The train is the local all-stations from Newcastle-upon-Tyne. Since privatisation this service terminates here rather than proceeding to Berwick-on-Tweed as hitherto; nevertheless, it has to run empty north to Belford (station closed in 1968) to find a crossover to enable the return journey to be operated. There are two southbound trains each day but only one north, the morning journey being empty stock. All very complicated!

△ The Post Bus stands in the grounds of the
INVERSNAID Hotel on the eastern shore of Loch
Lomond on 10 May 1996 with the great Bens on the
horizon. From here a ferry takes you to the main road
(the A82) to Tarbert and Crianlarich. To get here the
bus has run for miles along a lonely narrow road past
Lochs Chon and Arkles from Aberfoyle, very nice on
such a sunny day but misery in winter. Tourists often

come from the Trossachs across Loch Katrine on a
vintage boat.

▽ I believe that this service bus is acting as agent for
the Post Office in October 1975 at an unknown
location in the north of Scotland – sadly the details
are missing.

▽ This remote spot is not too far from Bridge of Orchy in northern Strathclyde. The Post 'Bus' is returning from the isolated community at **ACHALLADER** along an unsurfaced track on 13 May 1975.

▽ *Inset* On 30 August 1980 the Post 'Bus', again in the form of a private car, has arrived at its destination of **LAIRG** in Sutherland and awaits returning mail and passengers.

◁ On 21 April 1973 the Post Bus has reached its destination in **KINLOCHEWE** at the junction of the road from Loch Torridon and the A832 (Dingwall-Gairloch) from Achnasheen station on the railway to Skye. I wonder how many passengers it carried.

▽ To conclude this section is a famous scene on the island of **BARRA**, where the Post Bus has connected on the beach with the aircraft from the mainland at lunchtime on 2 May 1991. A Land Rover had been driven out into the sea half an hour earlier to remove any driftwood that might have endangered the landing.

Post Offices in
Wales

△ The name of this Post Office – **NORTON** – doesn't sound at all Welsh, but it is located in the principality between Knighton and Presteigne and so merits inclusion here. The picture was taken from the churchyard opposite on 6 April 1990.

▷ A post van bearing its Welsh credentials calls at **KINNERTON** where the postman empties the box at coffee time on 17 April 1991.

Two views – inside and outside – of
the Post Office at **ABERANGELL**
near Dolgelly, formerly in
Merioneth, on 20 August 1991. The
postmistress was very anxious that I
should photograph her pet goat!

A Post Office that looked very down-at-heel on 21 April 1993, **LLANDDEWI BREFI** is between Lampeter and Tregaron on the B4343. I, however, have come over the hills from Sarn and have seen no one for miles on very narrow twisting lanes through Coed Esgair Goch – very enjoyable and quite exciting on a sunny morning.

LLANDEILO boasts two Post Offices – the current one and its 1897 predecessor – seen on 24 July 2002 prior to lunch at The Cawdor Arms.

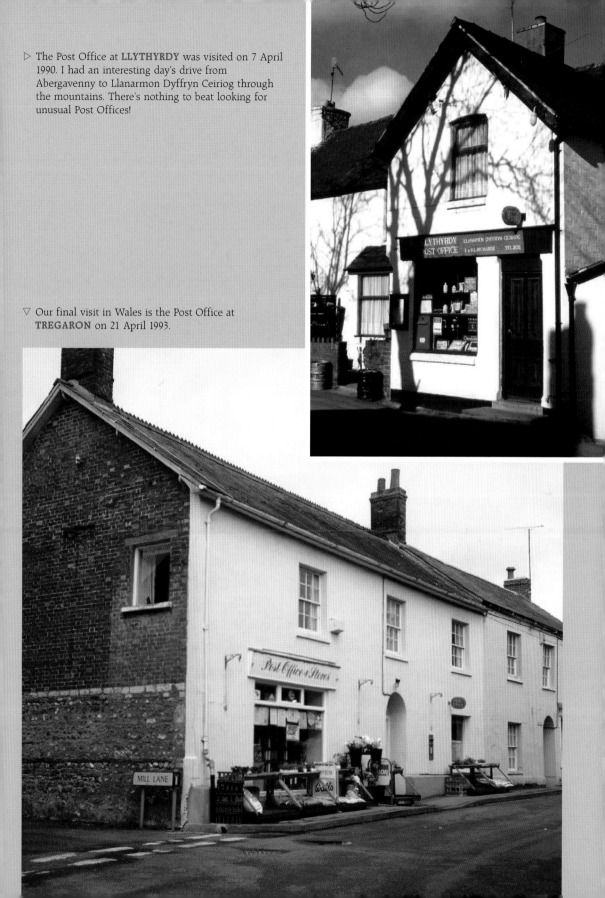

▷ The Post Office at **LLYTHYRDY** was visited on 7 April 1990. I had an interesting day's drive from Abergavenny to Llanarmon Dyffryn Ceiriog through the mountains. There's nothing to beat looking for unusual Post Offices!

▽ Our final visit in Wales is the Post Office at **TREGARON** on 21 April 1993.

Post Offices in
East Anglia

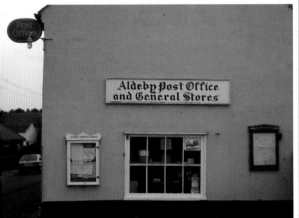

◁ North of the River Waveney and in a very low-lying peninsula threatened by the sea as global warming takes effect lies the village of **ALDEBY** whose Post Office and general stores marks our return to the East Coast on 14 August 1990.

▽ Much further north, and adjacent to the south side of the Humber estuary, stands **BARTON-UPON-HUMBER**, now overshadowed in part by the famous bridge uniting both parts of what became Humberside in 1974 and has since rejoined its older counties. The town remains the terminus of a railway branch line with a regular service to and from Grimsby and Cleethorpes.

▷ The Post Office at **BECCLES** is a superb building standing boldly in the main street. I'm on the upper floor of a shop to get a good view from the opposite side of the thoroughfare on 14 August 1990.

▷ The contrast in property used by the Royal Mail could hardly be better shown than the comparison of Beccles with **BLANKNEY** on the B1188 within the estate midway between Sleaford and Lincoln.

△ **EAST RUSTON** Post Office in Norfolk hides behind a screen of hedgerow near Cromer with its red telephone box proudly displayed on 15 August 1990.

▽ **LITCHAM** Post Office still carries its old-style enamel sign on 15 August 1990 and is a telegraph office. The location is on the B1145, which runs from east to west above Dereham and heads for King's Lynn, though that is quite far away. The wall box has seen some service over the years!

We have moved south through Dereham to reach **REYMERSTON**, about a mile west of the B1135 Dereham-Wymondham road, on 15 August 1990. Here we can see not only the façade with its dated advertisement for Lyons Tea but also inside with the charming postmistress and the well-stocked provisions before supermarkets came along and threatened this kind of business for those with access to a car.

◁ Near Diss we came across a Post Office in a modern house at **STOKE ASH**, which has nonetheless retained a sign from an earlier establishment. These two views are dated 13 August 1990.

▷ Into the Lincolnshire Wolds now, and to **SOUTH ORMSBY**, home of the Massingham Arms as well as a neat Post Office with charming windows. It is 2 May 1994.

▷ **THORNEY** Post Office is on my route from home to Cambridge and is just east of Peterborough. Until 1957 trains called here on their way to Yarmouth on the Midland & Great Northern Joint line, but today the level crossing gates are just ornaments in a nearby garden. The date is 1 September 1995.

◁ **WETHERINGSETT** in Suffolk was the first Post Office visited on the mammoth tour recorded in this book. The date is Monday 13 August 1990 and we have stayed overnight with friends in Felixstowe, whose home overlooks the sea near the mouth of the Stour and the Orwell; even then a procession of vessels was entering and leaving the expanding quaysides as well as those with Harwich as their port of call. We were surprised by the casual though professional nature of the Post Office, and it was a happy omen for our research. These three pictures seek to convey the atmosphere – the thatched exterior, the cat on the window sill and the handbell, which rang as customers arrived and left.

▽ Ten miles from Wetheringsett is **WORTHAM**, and again we are in the vicinity of Diss. It is later on the same day and expectations could not be higher. In the evening we are making our first visit to the Snape Maltings to hear the American organist Carlo Curley play Elgar; we are a bit apprehensive as to whether his overt and robust style will suit the sonata, but in the event all is well! After dark we cross the River Yare on the vehicular chain ferry at Reedham after summoning the boat from the pub across the water.

Before those events, however, we called at **FUNDENHALL** where the Post Office is located in a shed in the grounds of the manor house. I've included three pictures to convey the flavour of the place, which is off the B1113 about ten miles south-west of Norwich. We found the gates of the drive open and a side gate with an enamel sign in first-class condition. On pressing a push-button a bell could be heard ringing somewhere, but no one came. So I walked to a nearby filling station.

'Oh, mother's out exercising the dogs. She won't be long!' said the attendant.

Nor was she, and on her return she produced tea and cakes served in the parlour. This expedition was going to be good! This seems a good place to leave East Anglia and turn to the black and white archive photographs of the UK kindly supplied by the Post Office Museum & Archive.

Interlude
Post Offices from the archive

On 20 September 1989 I made my way for the first time to the Post Office Archive, then at Freeling House, 23 Glasshill Street, in South East London, overlooking the railway as it approached Blackfriars station from south of the river. Here I had the good fortune to meet Jean Farrugia, then the archivist. I could not have been made more welcome and when I explained the purpose of my visit every assistance was given to me and I was allowed free access to the photographic collection. I listed hundreds of pictures of possible interest and have gradually whittled these down to the best, in my opinion, which take up the next twenty pages. Naturally there have been significant changes to the administration of the Post Office since 1989 and the archives have been moved to Phoenix Place, but the assistance has remained of a high order and Barry Atto has dealt patiently and efficiently with my enquiries. The result is now for you to see with locations in alphabetical order. The dates of the views are stated where known.

This is **BELTON** Post Office in Norfolk (near Great Yarmouth) in 1947. The postman is chatting to the sub-postmaster, who is licensed to sell tobacco.

△ In 1965 **BEWDLEY** Post Office in Worcestershire had just been rebuilt at a cost of £27,022, providing a total gross area of 1,993 square feet. The style of building is typical of the area.

▽ This picture postcard shows Little Common Post Office at **BEXHILL**, East Sussex, on the A259 coast road just north of the famous Cooden Beach Hotel and a station where trains to and from London were bound to call at one time. The policeman stands head and shoulders above the children – I wonder what they have done? The date is not known.

Post Office, Little Common, Bexhill-on-Sea

Valentines Series 48073

POST OFFICE, BLEWBURY

◁ The official photographer has arrived at **BOVINGDON** in Hertfordshire and is probably concealed under his cloak with a large camera mounted on a tripod. Sadly neither of the two pictures shown here has a date, and they clearly illustrate two different buildings, although the signage has been transferred between them.

△ **BLEWBURY** is in Berkshire, on the A417 Reading-Wantage road.

▷ At **BOX** in Wiltshire – location of the famous tunnel on the Great Western Railway's Paddington to Bristol main line – it was the telegraph pole that took my eye and seemed worth recording.

At **BRADWELL-ON-SEA** in Essex the Post Office shares its frontage
with a veteran car; **BRIMPTON** is in Berkshire, near Newbury.

△ While in Essex, why not join the crowd of onlookers outside the Post Office on **CANVEY ISLAND**. Sadly there is no date or details of what is going on. The variety of dress is interesting, and not a woman in sight!

▽ It is May 1937 and we are admiring the Post Office at **GLYNDE** in East Sussex. The opera house at nearby Glyndebourne had opened three years earlier and the audience in their finery and carrying champagne hampers then came by special Pullman train from Victoria station in London. Clearly the shop has a wide range of provisions, as shown on the vintage metal advertisements.

▽ *Below* A very rural scene at **GRANGE** at the head of Derwent Water in the Lake District south of Keswick.

▽ *Bottom* This picture of **GREAT CANFIELD** is of interest not only for the ancient motorcycle but also the Dunmow Flitch chairs used in the ancient local ceremony of the bacon.

▷ It is April 1933 at **HUTTON** Post Office near Penrith in Cumbria. Someone is proud of their topiary work.

I just love this picture of the postman punting his boat along the River Nene while delivering mail to outlying farms in the fens near **GUYHIRN**, south-west of Wisbech.

▷ Although the date is May 1936
I am willing to gamble that little has changed
here at **KELD** in upper Swaledale, North Yorkshire.
The postman's round includes Tan Hill, with the
highest pub in England.

▽ A year later, come down the track with me to this
Post Office near **LOWESWATER** in the Lake District
– it's always time for a chat.

△ On page 79 we will visit the Post Office at Malpas in Cheshire, but here is **MALPAS** on the Truro River, almost due south of the city of Truro in Cornwall. It's March 1937 and the ferry is crossing the river.

▷ This picture is thought to have been taken in March 1918 and shows eight postmen (no women yet?) who made the rounds of **MARCH** in Cambridgeshire.

◁ I have included this picture at **NORTH PETHERTON** near Taunton in Somerset because of the vintage car.

By contrast **OAKHAM**'s Post Office (originally in Rutland, then Leicestershire, now Rutland again) is a fine and imposing building, seen on an unknown date. This is still a pleasant little town, but when I first stayed there in the 'fifties the water supply was cut off between 10.00pm and 6.00am with all the inconvenience that caused. Presumably Eye Water and other sources have mitigated this problem.

△ I have not included Northern Ireland in our UK itinerary, so was pleased to find two charming archive pictures taken there. The first is at **PARKMORE**, where the motorist has left his contemporary car to post a letter.

▷ I wonder what there is in the sack at **RATHLIN ISLAND** in September 1936...

△ This charming scene at **RADLEY** near Oxford is sadly not dated. Radley is almost a suburb of the city today.

◁ Many miles from Radley and near the Tees is **REDCAR** Post Office, again at an unknown date but showing its pedigree.

▷ *Above right* **ROYSTON** in Hertfordshire is seen in 1912. The Post Office is on the right and the road probably became the A505 from Baldock until the town bypass took away the through traffic.

▷ *Right* We move south of the Thames now to **SHIPBOURNE** near Sevenoaks in Kent and an interesting display of goods for sale in the sub-Post Office in 1935.

No. 134 - Royston - Melbourn Street.   Robert H. Clark's Series.

◁ *Left* The first of these two shop fronts in the London area is **SHAFTESBURY PARK**, SW. Once more the goods on display are of interest.

◁ *Below left* The second is in Knights Hill Road, **WEST NORWOOD**, with presumably Fred Hedger at the door. The politics in the press looks apprehensive.

▷ This Post Office is hard by Bristol's **TEMPLE MEADS** station, and looks more like a chapel.

▽ **TENDRING** in Essex is on the peninsula that also boasts Clacton, Frinton and Walton on the Naze within its neighbourhood. This vintage picture is dated 1910.

◁ *Left* The Post Office at **TILBURY DOCKS** in Essex is seen in 1908. On parade are Mr Henry Suggett, the postmaster, together with Misses Millie and Laura Suggett, counter clerks, on the right of their father. There are in addition five telegraph messengers and five postmen, and – please note – two female telegraphists! Mr Suggett also ran the confectionery shop.

◁ *Below left* What a contrast! **WANGFORD** is on the Norfolk/Suffolk border near Thetford.

I really like this archive picture. The coachman is waiting with a conveyance while his master has gone to deal with the mail. It is 22 June 1905 and the location is **WOODFORD GREEN** in Essex.

△ The next three archive pictures are in Scotland. The first is at **BERRIEDALE** on the east coast between Helmsdale and Wick – do notice the display of antlers along the roof line.

▽ Over on the west coast we are now at **BELLANOCH** on the Crinan Canal, a long way south of Oban. This canal connects Loch Fyne at Lochgilphead with the sea, was opened in 1801, and still remains navigable today.

▷ *Above right* South of Loch Lomond lies **DRYMEN**, and I could not resist this archive view with the vintage van and postmistress. The shop boasts a public telephone.

▷ *Right* Last but not least we move to Wales, and a somewhat newer picture. Here is the Post Office at **RHOS** near Haverfordwest in Pembrokeshire in May 1949. Perhaps they are chatting about a possible pictorial celebration of their profession!

Post boxes

This is a subject in its own right and I cannot do better than refer interested readers to *Old Letter Boxes* by Martin Robinson, published by Shire Publications Ltd of Princes Risborough in 1987.

That August Post Office Archives produced a comprehensive geographical list of where all the variations of Victorian boxes could be located, as well as those in a range of museums. Even then, this indicated a dozen types from the early non-standard examples of the 1850s to the cylindrical 'boxes' of 1887. A second sheet provided the whereabouts of the boxes bearing the cipher of King Edward VIII.

This small selection pales into insignificance by comparison, but this is a subject that cannot be overlooked in our pictorial survey.

▽ The wall box on the road to Kirkby Stephen at **BROUGH** in North Yorkshire was photographed on 18 February 1992. This village is on the A66 trans-Pennine road from Scotch Corner to Penrith and eastbound is the gateway to Stainmore, where the road is often subject to severe weather conditions and sometimes closed to all traffic.

▽ This is a Penfold box at **BUXTON** in Derbyshire on 25 March 1995. I'm on my way to Llangollen and have paused for a light lunch in the winter gardens run by High Peak Borough Council – in my experience always reliable and served in very agreeable circumstances!

◁ This box was located on **PULBOROUGH** station in Sussex in 1883 and is seen here on 3 March 1995. I've come to London for a Carmen's livery banquet at the Mansion House the previous evening, and have felt more than usually dim all day!

▽ Here is a box bearing King Edward VIII's cipher at **TOBERMORY** on the Isle of Mull, photographed on 9 May 1991.

Mail by rail

In November 1830, within a few days of the opening of the Liverpool & Manchester Railway, mail was being sent by train. Eight years later an experimental 'Travelling Post Office' was introduced on the Grand Junction Railway (Birmingham to Earlstown on the Liverpool & Manchester line) in which mails could be sorted and bagged up en route. Apparatus on the side of the coach and at the edge of the permanent way enabled mails to be picked up and offloaded while the train was in motion. Standardised equipment dates from 1852 and can still be seen today in active use on the preserved Nene Valley Railway near Peterborough. The first apparatus was sited at Boxmoor near Hemel Hempstead in 1838 and the last came out of service on the same West Coast Main Line at Penrith on the night of 14 October 1971.

Letter boxes were provided on trains from 1882, latterly consisting of a hinged flap and an aperture in the side of the coach. It is perhaps significant that the high cost of sending mails by rail caused the Post Office to reintroduce long-distance horse-drawn mail over some routes from London in 1887. History was to repeat itself a century later. In September 1988 a contract worth £45 million a year was signed between the Post Office and British Rail, and the Queen was pleased to mark the event with a visit to a Travelling Post Office at Worcester (Shrub Hill) station. However, the following year a railway strike disrupted deliveries and mail has been diverted to air and road. Large articulated vehicles had been tried in East Anglia in 1963. By 2008 there were only two or three regular mail trains and only on the West Coast Main Line between London, Warrington and Glasgow.

◁ The interior of a Travelling Post Office. *British Postal Museum & Archive*

▷ *Above right* Ex-LMS 'Jubilee' Class 4-6-0 No 45634 *Trinidad* passes mail pick-up apparatus on the West Coast Main Line. *Author's collection*

▷ *Right* Apparatus by the lineside with mail bags awaiting collection near Bletchley on the West Coast Main Line. *Author's collection*

△ Mail bags awaiting collection at Watford Junction.
Coaches of the Cheshire Lines Committee were being
used on outer London suburban services at the time.
Author's collection

▽ Mail bags on barrows at Euston station, photographed
through the window of a former London & North
Western Railway electric train. *Author's collection*

▷ This map dates from 1947 and was given to the
author by W. D. Taylor of the GPO during the 1965/66
session of the 'Talking of Trains' WEA evening class,
which he began at Surbiton in Surrey in 1960 and
which still exists after 47 years with its third
organiser; the author continues to 'preach' at Malton
in the heart of winter.

△ *Above* At 03.27 on Saturday 28 September 1996 electro-diesel locomotive No 73114 waits to leave Tonbridge in Kent with the last 9.00pm Manchester-Dover TPO. *Keith Dungate*

△ *Above right* A Royal Mail-liveried motor luggage van waits to leave Redhill for London Bridge on Sunday 7 May 1989. *Keith Dungate*

▽ Electro-diesel locomotives Nos 73107 *Redhill 1844-1994* and 73129 *City of Winchester* head the 1.26pm Tonbridge-Glasgow Central mails on 13 June 1994. The

train is heading towards Redhill and passing above the Oxted-Uckfield line in Edenbridge Tunnel, Kent. *Keith Dungate*

▷ *Right* Diesel-electric loco No 47787 calls at Reading with the 7.20pm Dover-Manchester TPO on 26 September 1996. *Keith Dungate*

▷ *Below right* A mail train formed of a third-rail electric multiple unit leaves Tonbridge at 1.47pm on 12 May 2003 bound for London via Sevenoaks.

◁ Just beyond Colton South Junction near York on 19 May 1995, this lightweight mail train to Leeds has two locomotives!

◁ Another electric multiple unit, but one powered by overhead electric wires, runs south along the West Coast Main Line at Carnforth in Lancashire at 3.30pm on 15 March 2001.

▽ Burnt Walls is east of Gilsland in Northumberland on the Newcastle-Carlisle line, and this Royal Mail special is carrying Lord Whitelaw home to Darlington from a postal ceremony in Carlisle on 6 September 1991.

▷ This mail train at Croxdale, on the East Coast Main Line south of Durham, is hauled in tandem by a diesel and an electric locomotive. The train originated at the postal depot near Newcastle and will reverse at Doncaster where the diesel locomotive will 'run round' the coaches, then head for Derby, avoiding Sheffield by using the original Midland main line to Chesterfield. The date is 3 April 1995.

△ The southbound postal service to Barrow-in-Furness
in Cumbria and beyond approaches Seascale in June
1972.

▽ Some years later, on 26 September 1988, the same
train stands in the far bay at Workington station.

△ This ex-Southern Railway TPO van carries the 'GR' cipher, and was photographed on the Nene Valley Railway. *Mike Esau*

△ Also on the Nene Valley was this EWS coach bearing the current Royal insignia. *Mike Esau*

▽ The 2.20pm Glasgow/Edinburgh-London postal via the East Coast Main Line is seen at Horn Burn, west of Ayton on the Scottish border, on 14 May 1996. This train used to run hard on the heels of the

4.00pm express from Edinburgh to King's Cross and even ran ahead sometimes, but probably only as far as the loop at Berwick on Tweed.

The Royal Mail TPO on the Nene Valley Railway at Wansford has its collection apparatus extended to pick up the two mail bags. *Mike Esau*

Post Offices in
The Midlands

▷ **MALPAS** Post Office in Cheshire, on the road from Whitchurch to Chester, is seen on 8 April 1990, which was a Sunday, hence the closed look about the premises!

▽ **ALMELEY**, south-east of Kington, was visited on 19 April 1991 during a relaxed day driving through the meadows of Herefordshire and the Welsh borders.

◁ **BRAMPTON BRYAN**, also in Herefordshire, is on the A4113, which connects Ludlow with Knighton. Here we have a Post Office on a busy road rather than in a hidden-away village. The date is 17 April 1991.

▽ The Golden Valley in Herefordshire lives up to its name, and the Post Office at **DORSTONE** looked in keeping when I visited on 20 April 1991. I had been spending a few days at The Radnorshire Arms in Presteigne, using it as a centre for a number of sorties to postal venues, and went home the next day. (I spent one morning in the hotel garden watching a gang of men erect a large marquee for a weekend event – very complicated and fascinating to observe!)

▷ The previous day I had been to three venues in Herefordshire; this is the Post Office at **EARDISLEY** with its clean looks and local architecture.

▽ Eardisley and **LYONSHALL**, on the A480 Hereford-Kington road, were once connected by a railway branch line that linked two secondary routes a few miles apart and was to suffer closure when wartime economies struck in July 1940. The date is 18 April 1991.

The post van at **STAUNTON ON ARROW**, Herefordshire, has come across the border from Wales and the postman is emptying English mail into his bag on 19 April 1991. The River Arrow connects the village with Kington and Leominster.

◁ *Inset* **SUTTON ST NICHOLAS** is a few miles north of Hereford and from the churchyard trains can be seen running between that city and Shrewsbury. I've come here on the same day between photographs at Moreton on Lugg, where a small industrial estate provides a lineside parking place for the car.

△ **WALTHAM ON THE WOLDS** in Leicestershire is midway between Melton Mowbray and Grantham, and the Post Office – seen here from the churchyard on 30 September 1989 – is down a lane to the east.

▷ Northamptonshire is a county less frequented by tourists and they miss a grand area, which I like to call the golden Cotswolds. **GRAFTON UNDERWOOD** stands away from the ironstone deposits but has a charm of its own, as seen here on 28 May 1998.

◁ Between Grafton Underwood and Weekley lies **WARKTON** with its thatched Post Office.

▽ On the same day I visited **WEEKLEY**. The thatch is glorious, as are the cakes!

▷ Watford Gap has become a famous place for refreshment on the M1 motorway, but the village of **WATFORD** itself stands quietly to the east on a small hill. On 1 September 1990 the Northamptonshire ironstone colour is much in evidence around the Post Office front door.

▽ By comparison the Post Office at **WHICHFORD**, near Hook Norton in Oxfordshire, looks quite austere.

△ **SOUTH LEVERTON** is in
Nottinghamshire, not far from
Retford to the west and Cottam
power station on the Trent to the
east. The date is 24 June 1994, and
as you can see the Post Office has
ended up as part of The Plough
public house – what a good idea!

◁ The Post Office at **HONINGTON**
is off the A34 south-east of
Stratford-upon-Avon, near
Shipston-on-Stour in
Warwickshire.

▷ The area of these two views is now a favourite haunt of mine on the Welsh border near Offa's Dyke. The first picture is at **BISHOP'S CASTLE**, where I like to acquire second-hand long-playing records and always enjoy a stroll down and up the hill with its market hall near the summit – a town of real character. The date is 3 April 1990.

▽ A few miles south is **CLUN**, Housman's quietest place under the sun, and I have crossed the River Clun to find the Post Office Stores on the same day. I have driven from a hotel at Great Longstone in Derbyshire to a farmhouse near Knucklas, west of Knighton on the Welsh border. What a lovely ride!

RATLINGHOPE, Shropshire, is a really isolated community under the western shoulder of the Long Mynd and miles south of Shrewsbury. The Post Office is in this grand house; opening hours were 9.00am until 1.00pm on Tuesdays and Thursdays only. My visit took place on 3 April 1990 en route to Bishop's Castle and Clun.

Post Offices in
Yorkshire

I called at the Post Office at **NORTH GRIMSTON**, south of Malton in North Yorkshire, one hot afternoon in 1990. It was Tuesday 25 September, and the Post Office was in the disused weighbridge house of the old railway station; trains to Malton and to Driffield and Bridlington had ceased to call there in 1950, though minerals from Burdale Quarry to Redcar had passed through for many years thereafter. A notice at the counter read 'Please pull this rope!' I then observed the said rope and, giving it a tug, heard a bell ring somewhere in the garden. Imagine my surprise when I discovered that the rope led to a handbell hanging on an old birdcage stand. This arrangement enabled the postmaster to enjoy his garden while being made conscious of any customers.

◁ **ALLERSTON** is east of Pickering on the Scarborough Road. I pass through there frequently, and this view was taken on 3 February 1992, a date when I visited a number of locations in the vicinity.

◁ In May 1974 I took a holiday at my then favourite retreat – Close House, Giggleswick – and was away from my home in Kingston-upon-Thames for twelve days. During that time I took this picture at **ARNCLIFFE** in the Dales and believe that the minivan is serving the Post Office, though this is not clear from the view. The date is almost certainly Thursday 16 May.

△ Comparatively nearby on foot but a long way by road through the hills is **BUCKDEN** at the head of Wharfedale. The B6160 provides links to Grassington and Aysgarth, though significant distances are involved. The date is 26 May 1990.

▷ **BURRILL** lies at the junction of three quiet lanes south-east of Bedale. It is 13 November 1992, and I saw the Redcar-Redmile ore train several times that day on the Wensleydale line from Northallerton, before the line was preserved.

CONISTON COLD lies on the A65 trunk road between Skipton and Hellifield and the Post Office used to be on the south side of the road. These two views are from the autumn of 1989.

DALTON is south of the A66 and north of Richmond in North Yorkshire, while **EAST WITTON** is a little further south and straddles a green running west towards Coverdale off the A6108; the Post Office is on the south side. The date is 3 July 1990, and I was making my way through hilly lanes from Coverdale to Wharfedale – a really scenic route.

△ **FARNDALE** is famous for its daffodils and tourists flock there in the spring. The Post Office is almost hidden by the flowers and foliage.

◁ The village of **GANTON** lies on the A64 York-Scarborough Road, and is more famous for its golf course than its Post Office, seen here on 26 February 1992. I remember that I began a sore throat in the evening, which developed into a real cold!

△ The Post Office at **HACKNESS** adjoins the church and lake adjacent to Lord Derwent's estate and is sited in a wooded valley in a beautiful location north-west of Scarborough. The picture dates from 3 February 1992.

▷ We are in South Yorkshire now and visiting the country Post Office at **HOOTON PAGNELL** on the B6422, which connects the village with Doncaster. I cannot trace the date of this picture.

△ The strangely named hamlet of **HORSEHOUSE** is on the narrow road through Carlton Highdale. which comes from Middleham and drops into Kettlewell in deepest North Yorkshire. This picture was taken from the churchyard on 3 July 1990.

◁ **KIRBY MISPERTON** is home to 'Flamingoland' and lies south-west of Pickering off the Malton Road. The bus from Leeds regularly diverts from the main road to run to and from the village by the same road and often picks up and sets down no passengers!

◁ **KIRKBY MALZEARD** is north-west of Ripon and boasts a number of streets. It is well away from any main road and there is little reason to pass through – rather stay and enjoy the atmosphere.

▽ **KIRKLINGTON** is well north of Ripon and less than two miles west of the A1, but is on a quiet road north that leads eventually to Bedale. It is 13 November 1992.

△ The Post Office at **LANGTON**, south of Malton, used to be just through
the estate gates (leading to a school), seen here in September 1975.

▽ **MASHAM** Post Office has moved premises several times, and on
20 November 1991 it was in an old church hall, but well sited for the little
town.

Two villages in North Yorkshire share the same name. This is **MELMERBY** above Wensleydale and south of West Witton on the Leyburn-Hawes Road, located on the lane to Horsehouse already seen above. The date is 3 July 1990.

△ The second **MELMERBY** is near Ripon, photographed on the same day as its namesake.

◁ **RAVENSCAR** Post Office looks as though it could be in a street in a north London suburb rather than by the coast and in wild country, especially in winter. The picture was taken on 3 February 1992 but it looks like a spring day!

I came across the Post Office at **STAINTONDALE** by chance on 3 February 1992, as it was not on my checklist – it was the sign that brought it to my notice. When I stopped outside the little double-fronted cottage I could see the lady in charge doing some washing-up in the window. She welcomed me in and I came away with a jar of home-made marmalade. She also said that I should visit a relative who ran the Post Office in the unlikely named village of Whitchurch Canonicorum. Little did she expect me to be in Dorset shortly afterwards, so I turned up there, much to the old lady's delight (see page 20).

◁ Nearby to the south-east is **SCALBY**, which heralds the approach to Scarborough. I was there soon after visiting Ravenscar on 3 February 1992.

▽ **THORNTON WATLASS** is located west of the Bedale-Masham Road and is lost in the pastoral meadowland there. The date is 3 July 1990.

THORNTON-LE-DALE on the A170
is a tourist honeypot and is always
busy at all times of the year. The
Post Office there is seen on
6 September 2005. *Keith Dungate*

△ **THWAITE** is in upper Swaledale near the junction of the valley road with that over the Butter Tubs from Hawes. It really is picturesque and has all the attributes of the copybook country village. The Post Office is on the left, next door to the pub.

◁ My last picture in Yorkshire is at **WEST WITTON**, a main-road village on the way from Leyburn to Hawes in Wensleydale.

Post Offices in
The North Country

I began my itinerary at **ROWELTOWN** on a minor road some miles north of Brampton in Cumbria. The Post Office was in a farmyard and here the post vans assembled before making their lonely journeys around the difficult terrain of the border country. The building faces north, and I asked one of the farm workers whether the sun ever shone on it. He said that it did early on a July morning, and that if I came back at such a time he would lend me a ladder so that I could climb on to the roof of one of the cowsheds to get a better view. I have yet to take him up on this idea. The date is 14 October 1991.

I have included four illustrations of the Post Office at
MUNGRISDALE near Keswick in the Lake District
because of its interest in my itinerary.

It is situated in an old school and open only for two
hours on Tuesday and Thursday afternoons. I arrived
there on 15 October 1991 with David Short at twenty
minutes to three o'clock to find the sign on the garden
gate reading 'closed'. Nevertheless we decided to venture
into the garden only to find an elderly lady almost
hidden in the shrubbery. Miss Dorothy Chalk was clearly
distressed lest we were officials from Post Office HQ – it
transpired that for the first time in her thirty years as
postmistress she had shut herself out of the building
and that the spare keys were with a neighbour who was
not expected home for another hour or so. When we
explained the reason for our visit there was obvious
relief! In due course the building was unlocked and we
found it to be filled with bric-a-brac, crockery, lamp
shades and the like. She explained that she was a bit of
a hoarder and that last time she had cleared the place
village funds had benefited to the tune of £2,500!

△ Whenever I go to Farlam Hall Hotel near Brampton in Cumbria I take myself to the hamlet of **BEWCASTLE** en route to the borders and Scotland. As you can see, the Post Office there is in a little green hut just off the road. It is 16 May 1992 and I am on my way to Biggar near Peebles in Scotland.

▽ But then there is the city of **CARLISLE** to visit, so I include one Post Office in a residential area.

▽ Changed priorities near **NEWBY BRIDGE** in Cumbria on 9 April 1989. Concern for the environment personified!

△ **PORT CARLISLE** is one of many examples where the Post Office has moved into the village pub. I had a drink and a slice of cake after taking this picture on 14 October 1989. (I'm on a weekend course at Higham Hall near Cockermouth and have ventured out during a free period.)

▷ Far to the east of the above picture – in Northumberland – lies the small town of **BELLINGHAM**. The first time I came here was in 1959 on a freight train from Morpeth, reversing at Reedsmouth on to the Border Counties Line (Hexham-Scotland), which had closed in 1956 but had been retained for a few miles to Bellingham. It seemed far away from home, and still does!

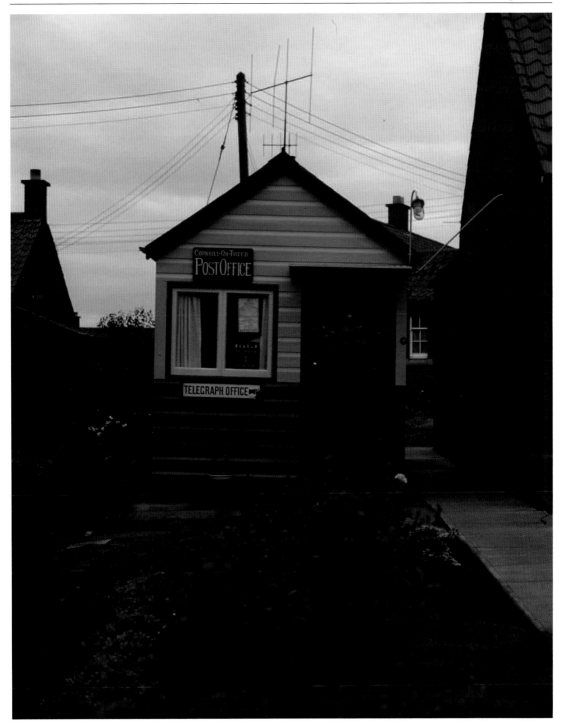

◁ This 5 August 1994 view of **CHATHILL** Post Office completes the set of pictures seen earlier on page 27 in the 'Post routes and Post Buses' section.

△ This little Post Office at **CORNHILL-ON-TWEED** was photographed on 28 August 1974, long before the idea came for this book, though I possibly had an inkling. Across the river lies Coldstream in Scotland.

△ When I called on 28 July 1989 they were trying to save their Post Office at **CAPHEATON** – I know not whether they were successful. The location is just south of the A696 Newcastle-Jedburgh road near the crossroads for the National Trust property at Wallington.

▽ Before we enter Scotland let's go off the East Coast to **HOLY ISLAND** on 5 August 1994. Tide tables have to be consulted if you are not to be marooned there when the tide comes in and covers the causeway from the mainland.

Post Offices in
Scotland

△ In my itinerary to locate different Post Offices I not
only toured mainland Scotland but also visited some
of the outer islands and met some very nice helpful
folk. I have decided to list the mainland Offices in
alphabetical order for ease of reference. Thus we
begin with **ARISAIG** at the head of Loch nan Ceall
(by which means Bonnie Prince Charlie made one of
his escapes!) on the road (and railway) from Fort
William to Mallaig. I have yet to see again the large
number of different whiskies available in the pub
there. It is 26 August 1993.

▷ Next is **BALQUHIDDER** between Callander and
Crianlarich on 21 August 1992. It was a railway
junction for Crieff and is at the head of Loch Earn,
which runs to the east.

△ **BEATTOCK**, on the A74(M) and the West Coast Main Line, is the gateway to the Lowther Hills, and the Post Office is in a small lodge, as seen here on 11 May 1995.

▽ A more formal building houses the Post Office at **CALLANDER**, as befits a significant town. It is 21 August 1992, and earlier in the day I had travelled across Loch Katrine in the Trossachs on a vintage boat whose ownership has changed hands frequently in line with national politics.

▷ One of the traditional signposts leads to the Post Office at **CAWDOR** in August 1993.

▷ Inset **GATEHEAD** is situated on the A759 west of Kilmarnock and had a railway station until 1969, although trains still pass this way between Newcastle and Stranraer, for example. It's 1 July 1991 and I'm staying with friends at Low Coylton near Ayr and see one of the first trains on the branch to leave the New Caledonian Paper Mills at Barassie on its long journey to Burngullow near St Austell in Cornwall to collect a further load of china clay. This traffic is now carried by sea.

▷ **HOWNAM** is in the Cheviot Hills and the Kale Water Valley, a long way south of Kelso. To make a through journey by car it is necessary to turn west here and head for Carter Bar on the A68 – a ride through wonderful country (on a fine day!). The date is 26 July 1989.

▽ **LEADHILLS** is descriptive of the neighbourhood, and mineral traffic used to be carried to the West Coast Main Line by the branch long closed to all traffic. There is a notable museum of local industry here. The photo dates from 18 May 1992.

△ On 21 August 1992 the Post Office at **LOCHEARNHEAD** looked like this. It is on the A85 from Callander to Crianlarich (or branch to Killin) at the south end of Glen Ogle.

▷ Tartan is the theme at **LUSS** Post Office on the west side of Loch Lomond. Regrettably this photograph is undated.

▽ **MONIAIVE** is on the A702 Thornhill-New Galloway road at the head of Cairn Water and is a favourite port of call for me before heading west into the lonely hills. This picture was taken in the autumn of 1994.

▽ **OBAN** is too well known to need any introduction, and the Post Office is of a style to befit this busy port and terminus of the railway from Glasgow. The date is 1 May 1991 and we will shortly join the boat that leaves late in the afternoon for the Island of Barra, where we are due at the hotel at 10.00pm. It proved to be a lovely sunny evening and became most memorable as we glided through the Sound of Mull. The only disappointment was the catering. In earlier years fresh fish would be cooked on board, and smelled and tasted delicious. Now some frozen item was heated up and served without any decorum.

▷ The population of **OXNAM** could not be more different from that of Oban! We've returned to the Cheviot Hills and the road from Hownam to which we referred on page 116. It's 26 July 1989.

▽ It so happens that I was staying nearby when the Post Office at **ROTHIEMAY** closed for the last time at 1.00pm on Wednesday 3 September 2008; the battle had come to a sad end here. The full name of the hamlet is Milltown of Rothiemay, and the picture was taken on 14 September 1992.

◁ **SANQUHAR** lays claim to have the oldest Post Office in the UK. An entry in the *Edinburgh Almanac* of 1763 states that the post left there on Saturday evenings at 9.00pm arriving back in Edinburgh the following Friday afternoon. The postage on a letter between Edinburgh and Sanquhar was then 2d, a single letter being one made up of a single sheet of paper, folded, sealed and the address written on the outside. By 1788 Sanquhar was receiving post from Edinburgh three times a week, but the postage had risen to 5d. The village stands astride the A76 Dumfries-Kilmarnock road in the Nith Valley, and is seen here on 30 April 1991.

▽ **STRATHCARRON** Post Office is immediately outside the railway station on the line from Inverness/Dingwall to the Kyle of Lochalsh. There are antlers on the platform. The picture dates from 25 August 1993.

▷ Now to the islands! **LAMLASH** is on the Isle of Arran off the Ayrshire coast and is reached by boat frequently between Ardrossan and Brodick. The view from the Post Office window is south-east across a grassy meadow and the bay to Holy Island. It's glorious! The date is 1 May 1991.

One of the Post Offices reached by air (see page 30) is that on **BARRA**. It is the next day in May, Thursday the 2nd, and we have come here on the evening boat from Oban with the car. The inset shows its title in Gaelic.

◁ Adjacent to the boat jetty at **TARBERT** on Harris are these containers for the Royal Mail.

▽ While touring Barra we visited the Post Office at **BRUERNISH** on the east coast – rather bleak here, even on 2 May 1991.

This is the Post Office at **AMHUINNSUIOH** on the Isle of Lewis on 4 May 1991. The waters of Loch Leosavay lap at the foundations and the sea lies beyond. The inset shows the Post Office on **IONA**.

Four pictures now on the Isle of Mull: first is the timber shed Post Office at **LOCH GON** in May 1991 (*left*). **PENNYGHAEL** (*right*) is south-east of Loch Scridain on the road to Iona. Notice the Land Rover to combat the poor roads to outlying properties. **TIRORAN** (*below and bottom*) is on the other side of the loch and was famed at one time for its entry in *The Good Food Guide*.

This is the Post Office at **TOBERMORY** (also on Mull, and home of the Edward VIII pillar box seen on page 67).

Back on Barra, this is the Post Office at **BORVE** on the west coast.

Finally, on 3 May 1991 we visit **STONEY BRIDGE** on South Uist, a couple of miles west of the spine road and dominated by Ben Mhor. This remote spot seems to me a suitable place to end our itinerary, which I hope you have enjoyed as much as myself.

Index of featured Post Offices